Popular Rock Superstars of Yesterday and Today

POP ROCK

AC/DC	Elton John
Aerosmith	The Grateful Dead
The Allman Brothers Band	Led Zeppelin
The Beatles	Lynyrd Skynyrd
Billy Joel	Pink Floyd
Bob Marley and the Wailers	Queen
Bruce Springsteen	The Rolling Stones
The Doors	U2
	The Who

The Allman Brothers Band

Peter Gregory

Mason Crest Publishers

The Allman Brothers Band

FRONTIS The Allman Brothers Band was an innovator in the rock scene. Southern rock and the Allman Brothers became synonymous.

Produced by 21st Century Publishing and Communications, Inc.

Editorial by Harding House Publishing Services, Inc.

MASON CREST PUBLISHERS INC.
370 Reed Road
Broomall, Pennsylvania 19008
(866) MCP-BOOK (toll free)
www.masoncrest.com

Printed in the United States.

First Printing

9 8 7 6 5 4 3 2 1

Library of Congress Cataloging-in-Publication Data

Gregory, Peter, 1956–
    The Allman Brothers Band / Peter Gregory.
        p. cm. — (Popular rock superstars of yesterday and today)
    Includes bibliographical references and index.
    Hardback edition: ISBN-13: 978-1-4222-0188-6
    Paperback edition: ISBN-13: 978-1-4222-0310-1
    1. Allman Brothers Band—Juvenile literature. 2. Rock musicians—United States—Juvenile literature. I. Title.
ML3930.A43G74 2008
782.42166092'2—dc22
[B]   2007019386

Publisher's notes:
- All quotations in this book come from original sources, and contain the spelling and grammatical inconsistencies of the original text.

- The Web sites mentioned in this book were active at the time of publication. The publisher is not responsible for Web sites that have changed their addresses or discontinued operation since the date of publication. The publisher will review and update the Web site addresses each time the book is reprinted.

CONTENTS

ROCK 'N' ROLL TIMELINE

1951
"Rocket 88," considered by many to be the first rock single, is released by Ike Turner.

1952
DJ Alan Freed coins and popularizes the term "Rock and Roll," proclaimes himself the "Father of Rock and Roll," and declares, "Rock and Roll is a river of music that has absorbed many streams: rhythm and blues, jazz, rag time, cowboy songs, country songs, folk songs. All have contributed to the Big Beat."

1955
"Rock Around the Clock" by Bill Haley & His Comets is released; it tops the U.S. charts and becomes wildly popular in Britain, Australia, and Germany.

1967
The Monterey Pop Festival in California kicks off open air rock concerts.

1965
The psychedelic rock band, the Grateful Dead, is formed in San Francisco.

1969
The Woodstock Music and Arts Festival attracts a huge crowd to rural upstate New York.

1969
Tommy, the first rock opera, is released by British rock band The Who.

1970
The Beatles break up.

1971
Jim Morrison, lead singer of The Doors, dies in Paris.

1971
Duane Allman, lead guitarist of the Allman Brothers Band, dies.

1950s   1960s   1970s

1957
Bill Haley tours Europe.

1957
Jerry Lee Lewis and Buddy Holly become the first rock musicians to tour Australia.

1954
Elvis Presley releases the extremely popular single "That's All Right (Mama)."

1961
The first Grammy for Best Rock 'n' Roll Recording is awarded to Chubby Checker for *Let's Twist Again*.

1964
The Beatles make their first visit to America, setting off the British Invasion.

1969
A rock concert held at Altamont Speedway in California is marred by violence.

1969
The Rolling Stones tour America as "The Greatest Rock and Roll Band in the World."

1973
Rolling Stone magazine names Annie Leibovitz chief photographer and "rock 'n' roll photographer;" she follows and photographs rockers Mick Jagger, John Lennon, and others.

1974
Sheer Heart Attack by the British rock band Queen becomes an international success.

1974
"Sweet Home Alabama" by Southern rock band Lynyrd Skynyrd is released and becomes an American anthem.

1987
Billy Joel becomes the first American rock star to perform in the Soviet Union since the construction of the Berlin Wall.

2005
Led Zeppelin is ranked #1 on VH1's list of the 100 Greatest Artists of Hard Rock.

1985
Rock stars perform at Live Aid, a benefit concert to raise money to fight Ethiopian famine.

2005
Many rock groups participate in Live 8, a series of concerts to raise awareness of extreme poverty in Africa.

2003
Led Zeppelin's "Stairway to Heaven" is inducted into the Grammy Hall of Fame.

1980
John Lennon of the Beatles is murdered in New York City.

2000s
Aerosmith's album sales reach 140 million worldwide and the group becomes the bestselling American hard rock band of all time.

2007
Billy Joel become the first person to sing the National Anthem before two Super Bowls.

1975
Tommy, the movie, is released.

1975
Time magazine features Bruce Springsteen on its cover as "Rock's New Sensation."

1995
The Rock and Roll Hall of Fame and Museum opens in Cleveland, Ohio.

1970s   1980s   1990s   2000s

1979
Pink Floyd's *The Wall* is released.

1991
Freddie Mercury, lead vocalist of the British rock group Queen, dies of AIDS.

2004
Elton John receives a Kennedy Center Honor.

1979
The first Grammy for Best Rock Vocal Performance by a Duo or Group is awarded to The Eagles.

2004
Rolling Stone Magazine ranks The Beatles #1 of the 100 Greatest Artists of All Time, and Bob Dylan #2.

1986
The Rolling Stones receive a Grammy Lifetime Achievement Award.

1981
MTV goes on the air.

2006
U2 wins five more Grammys, for a total of 22–the most of any rock artist or group.

1986
The first Rock and Roll Hall of Fame induction ceremony is held; Chuck Berry, Little Richard, Ray Charles, Elvis Presley, and James Brown, are among the first inductees.

1981
For Those About to Rock We Salute You by Australian rock band AC/DC becomes the first hard rock album to reach #1 in the U.S.

2006
Bob Dylan, at age 65, releases *Modern Times* which immediately rises to #1 in the U.S.

Dressed in finery befitting the occasion—and more fancy than usual—Gregg Allman (left) and Dickey Betts (right) show off their awards as 1995 inductees into the Rock and Roll Hall of Fame. The Allman Brothers Band was recognized for its influence on the history and development of rock music.

1

Getting Their Dues

S ome might have thought it was an odd-looking bunch to have gathered at the Waldorf-Astoria in January 1995. After all, the hotel was used to lavish parties and receptions attended by the cream of high society. But on this night, the hotel's ballroom was filled with another type of cream—the cream of the crop of the rock world.

For some of the musicians, such a fancy location made them feel uncomfortable. In appreciation of the honor being bestowed upon them, some traded in their more customary—and comfy—jeans and T-shirts for suits, and in some cases even ties, and flowing hair was stylishly **coiffed**. Everyone was on their best behavior, something more easily accomplished by some than others!

Choosing Who Goes Into the Hall

On January 13, 1995, for the tenth time, the Rock and Roll Hall of Fame was honoring the individuals and groups who had made a difference in rock music. Each honoree had to fulfill a specific **criteria** before being considered for election into the hall. For example, musicians first become eligible twenty-five years after their first recording. A nominating committee then decides who among the eligible have made significant contributions to the rock scene. Finally, the candidates' names are placed on ballots sent to writers and experts in the music business. The votes of these music experts determine who is **inducted** into the hall. Only between five and seven performers are elected each year.

Those inducted on that January night in 1995 had met the Rock and Roll Hall of Fame's requirements to be placed on the ballot, and they had passed the **scrutiny** of those casting the yes or no votes that meant entry into the hall or the need to wait another year. The newest members of the hall now included Al Green, Frank Zappa, Martha and the Vandellas, Janis Joplin, Led Zeppelin, Neil Young, and the Allman Brothers Band.

The Red-Headed Stranger Presents the Allman Brothers Band

Each inductee into the hall is presented by another person involved in the music industry. Sometimes the inductee and the presenter have a direct connection; other times, the presenter is just a fan. Country artist Willie Nelson—also called the Red-Headed Stranger—is an admitted fan who had the honor of presenting the band at its induction ceremonies. In his presentation, Willie spoke about the band's characteristics that meant the most to him:

> **"The Allman Brothers Band were and still are one of the most exciting live bands ever to hit the stage. They became road warriors with a vengeance and left devoted fans wherever they went. [The Allman Brothers Band is] a band that reflects so many of my sentiments about music: originality, a determination not to be confined musically or stylistically but instead to forge your own way and make music that**

Willie Nelson, a big fan of the Allman Brothers Band, had the honor of presenting the group at the Rock and Roll Hall of Fame induction ceremony in 1995. During his presentation speech, Willie called the Allman Brothers Band "one of the most exciting live bands ever to hit the stage."

moves you, a devotion to the road, and understanding that beyond pleasing yourself as an artist, the only other consideration should be the people, the fans who come to hear you.**"**

When interviewed before the ceremonies, Butch Trucks, the group's drummer, admitted the members had been somewhat surprised at the honor:

"We don't win awards or Grammys, so we were surprised when we got nominated. I think we all have a basic insecurity complex and like to win awards in order to feel like people accept us. But this award is important, plus it's a nice party."

The more than 1,000 gathered for the "nice party" were treated to an Allman Brothers Band performance of their classic "One Way Out."

In September 1995, it was the Allman Brothers Band's turn to honor the Rock and Roll Hall of Fame. After many years, the Hall of Fame was finally ready to open, and the Allman Brothers Band joined such rock icons as Bruce Springsteen, Little Richard, and Chuck Berry at the Concert for the Rock and Roll Hall of Fame.

But the induction ceremony wasn't the group's only involvement with the Rock and Roll Hall of Fame in 1995.

Opening the Hall

For many years, a home for the Rock and Roll Hall of Fame remained a dream. There were plans to build it in Cleveland, Ohio, but it seemed to be taking a very long time. Cleveland was chosen as the site for the hall in 1986, but groundbreaking didn't begin until 1993. Finally, in September 1995, it was ready, and the rock world was ready to give the hall a worthy welcome.

Some of the biggest names in rock came together for the Concert for the Rock and Roll Hall of Fame, held at Cleveland's Municipal Stadium. Chuck Berry and his guitar Lucille performed, as did Bruce Springsteen, Little Richard, Iggy Pop, and the Allman Brothers Band, one of the hall's newest inductees.

Each honoree in the Rock and Roll Hall of Fame has its own space. Videos of memorable performances are shown, and photos of the individuals and groups are exhibited. Visitors can read biographies of the musicians while watching performances.

The Rock and Roll Hall of Fame says of the Allman Brothers Band:

"the principal architects of Southern rock, the Allman Brothers Band . . . help advance rock as a medium for improvisation. Their kind of jamming required a level of technical virtuosity and musical literacy that was relatively new to rock and roll, which had theretofore largely been a song-oriented medium. . . . the Allman Brothers Band were a blues-rocking powerhouse from their beginnings in 1969."

Though the members of the Allman Brothers Band might disagree with the tag "Southern rock," the fact that they were innovators on the rock scene cannot be argued. The story of the Allman Brothers Band began with two brothers in Jacksonville, Florida.

Florida brothers Gregg and Duane Allman shared a dream—to play in a rock group. With Gregg on keyboards and Duane on guitar, the brothers were inspired by the success of the Beatles and other rock stars. Thanks to their hard work and obvious talent, the brothers were able to reach that dream.

2

Allman Joys to Allman Brothers

Almost every young person wanted to be a rock star in the 1960s. And who could blame them, especially after the Beatles and other members of the British Invasion hit the shores and airwaves of the United States. Though fame, fortune, and screaming fans were important to some, others just wanted to play their music.

Duane and Gregg Allman grew up in Jacksonville, Florida. Gregg, the younger of the two, was a talented guitarist who taught Duane how to play. Duane was a fast study, and Gregg encouraged his older brother to play and to learn more about the instrument and the sounds that he could get from it. Gregg was very persuasive; Duane dropped out of school so that he could become a guitar master. (That might not have been exactly what Gregg had in mind though.)

Allman Brothers—The Early Years

With Gregg on vocals and playing the organ and Duane on guitar, the two Allman brothers began their musical careers playing in garage bands around the Jacksonville and Daytona Beach areas in 1961. **Blues** and **soul** were their biggest influences during the early years, but once the British Invasion hit, they joined the millions of others who listened to the Rolling Stones, the Beatles, the Yardbirds, and other British bands. The brothers' first band was called the Escorts, and listeners couldn't help but note the influence of British bands, especially the Beatles and the Rolling Stones.

The Escorts didn't find the big time, so Gregg and Duane formed a band called the Allman Joys. Instead of the Beatles-style rock that had influenced the Escorts, the Allman Joys featured a return to the Allmans' first love—the blues. At the time, one of the most popular groups coming from Britain was Cream, featuring Eric Clapton, another master guitar player whose music had a more bluesy sound. The Allman Joys were influenced by Cream's sound.

Though their name was catchy, the Allman Joys failed to sign with a record company. Unwilling to give up on a music career, Gregg and Duane formed Hour Glass. Gregg and Duane turned now to one of their other favorite music styles—this time, soul. Now, their music finally caught on. Members of the Nitty Gritty Dirt Band heard Hour Glass play, and according to Jeff Hanna of the Dirt Band, they "were blown away." They convinced the guys to come to California, where the Dirt Band helped them get a contract with Liberty Records.

Liberty Records—Not So Free

The Allman brothers and the other members of Hour Glass learned some important lessons while they were with Liberty Records: record companies want hits, and they want them big, fast, and done their way.

As Hour Glass played gigs in California, they developed quite an impressive following. Besides "regular" fans, other bands would come to listen to them play. Buffalo Springfield, one of the biggest groups as the 1960s came to an end, was a big fan of Hour Glass and their soulful sound.

Despite the brothers' successful gigs, Liberty Records wanted Hour Glass to put aside their tried-and-true sound when it came to making an album. Hoping to hop on the pop bandwagon associated with the

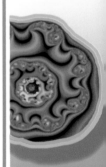

One of Gregg (back, center) and Duane's (front, left) first tries at rock stardom was with Hour Glass. They got a record contract, but it came with strings attached. The record company had its own ideas about how the group should make music, and those ideas didn't jive with the band's goals.

British Invasion, the record company had Hour Glass cut a more pop-oriented album. According to the Nitty Gritty Dirt Band's Jeff Hanna,

> **"They had the same record producer that we did and I don't know if I should blame it all on him or just corporate short-sightedness in the record business at that time. They didn't *get* what they did and they were not able to make the record that they should have."**

Hour Glass's first album was not a success, and neither was their second. Still, the guys were not ready to give up. The band had ideas for a third album, one that better reflected the blues and soul roots of the group, the type of music that people had come out to hear. Liberty wasn't interested. They knew what they wanted from Hour Glass, and blues and soul didn't fit into their equation. Liberty Records rejected the group's proposal. It also rejected Hour Glass and released all but Gregg from their contract. Liberty thought Gregg had potential as a vocalist and keyboardist and wanted to keep him tied to the label.

From Los Angeles to Muscle Shoals

With their dreams of a hot recording career shattered, Hour Glass broke up when Liberty released them. With Gregg committed to staying in Los Angeles to fulfill his contractual obligations with Liberty, Duane went back to Florida, with a stop in Muscle Shoals, Alabama.

As hard as it might be to believe, one of the hotbeds of the music industry in the 1960s and 1970s was far from bright lights and big cities. Muscle Shoals, Alabama, population of less than 15,000, was well on its way to earning a reputation as a music capital in the late 1960s and early 1970s. The biggest names in rock, soul, and blues—the Rolling Stones, Bob Dylan, Paul Simon, Boz Skaggs, Rod Stewart, and others—found their way to Fame Studios. No one can say with certainty why Muscle Shoals attracted so many big names and turned out such important recordings. According to Bruce Borgerson, who has written several articles about the phenomenon:

> **"It defies credibility. Muscle Shoals certainly lacked great hotels, fine restaurants, fast-paced night-life**

During the 1960s and 1970s, Muscle Shoals became a rock mecca. The biggest names in music found their way to the small Alabama town to record at Fame Studios. The Rolling Stones, Paul Simon, Rod Stewart, and Bob Dylan (shown here) all traveled to Muscle Shoals, where they found "100 proof Alabama honky soul."

(make that any night-life), or miles of sun-drenched tropical beaches. No, instead Muscle Shoals' sole drawing card to rock's elite was a peculiar musical culture that somehow bred musicians gifted with funky chops, steely determination, an open musical mind, and a rare commodity called 100 proof Alabama honky soul.**"**

Duane Allman was another musician who ended up at Muscle Shoals's Fame Studios. He became a well-respected session musician whose services were in high demand by rock superstars. And Duane worked with the biggest stars—Aretha Franklin and Wilson Picket, for example. With Duane on guitar, an artist knew the recording would be phenomenal.

Duane quickly found success as a session musician in Shoals. He worked with the big names—Aretha Franklin, Wilson Picket, King Curtis, and Johnny Jenkins. By 1969, he had developed the reputation as *the* person to get if you wanted the best guitarist for a recording session. Jerry Wexler of Atlantic Records said of Duane:

> **"He was a complete guitar player. He could do everything: play rhythm, lead, blues, slide, bossa-nova, with a jazz feeling, beautiful light acoustic—and on slide guitar he got *the* touch. Duane is one of the greatest guitar players I ever knew and one of the very few who could hold his own with the best of the black blues players."**

Back to Jacksonville

Despite his success, Duane eventually returned to Jacksonville and hooked up with other musicians in the area: guitarist Dickey Betts and bass player Berry Oakley of Second Coming and drummer Butch Trucks of the 31st of February. Drummer Johnny Lee Johnson, better known as Jaimoe, whom Duane had jammed with in Muscle Shoals, eventually joined them as well. Jaimoe was a veteran of the music scene. Like Duane, he had played with some of the biggest names on the music scene, including soul legend Otis Redding. His experience—and his talent—led to an easy fit with the others.

Duane, Dickey, Berry, Butch, and Jaimoe got together and did what most musicians do—they jammed. After a five-hour jam session, they knew they had something special, something worth building on. Their sound certainly had many influences. Second Coming—Dickey and Berry's band—specialized in psychedelic rock. But Dickey's musical background was really in country swing.

Country swing, also called Western swing, was a **fusion** of country music (then called country-western), jazz, pop, and blues. It was music meant to be danced to. Some of the big country swing names are Smokey Wood and the Wood Chips, the Washboard Wonders, and Bill Haley and the Saddlemen (although he's most remembered for the Comets).

Meanwhile, Berry's musical background was the Chicago blues. Butch, Jaimoe, and Duane had many influences on which to draw,

including blues, soul, and pop, though they were most attracted to rhythm and blues.

Despite how good they sounded together, they were still missing something. Duane knew exactly what it was—or rather, who it was: Gregg. He called his brother and told him to get to Florida. With the added lure of a Hammond organ to play, Gregg complied. On March 25, 1969, the Allman Brothers Band officially came into being.

Introducing the Allman Brothers Band

The band traveled and played around the South, building a fan base and fine-tuning their sound. They signed a recording contract with Capricorn, a relative newcomer on the music scene, and the band

Still looking to form his own group, Duane returned to Florida and met other musicians with the same goals. Jamming together, the guys found a sound they liked. So they jammed some more, and things just seemed to click. Almost. They still needed a vocalist and keyboard player. They needed Gregg.

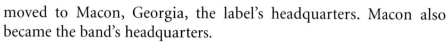

moved to Macon, Georgia, the label's headquarters. Macon also became the band's headquarters.

Times were sometimes tough for the guys in Macon. To save money, and to make it easier to jam whenever they wanted, they shared a house. Money was tight, and had it not been for "Mama Louise" Hudson and the H&H Restaurant, the guys wouldn't have eaten a whole lot—but Mama was generous with free meals.

Some people in Macon must have thought these guys were a strange bunch. Not many living in Macon had such long hair or played music so loudly. And then there was the whole cemetery thing. Sometimes at night (of course), the guys walked down to Rose Hill Cemetery, where they would practice among the tombstones to a, well, captive audience.

In 1969, the group released their debut album, *The Allman Brothers Band*. Critics praised the album—and the band—for its mix of rock, jazz, country, and blues. Unfortunately, critics aren't the major record buyers, and the album wasn't a big hit with the music-buying public. It has, however, become a cult classic and a must-have for any true fan of the Allman Brothers Band.

Though their recording career was off to a shaky start, it wouldn't take long before the Allman Brothers Band hit its stride and paved the way for a brand-new musical style.

"they would tour anywhere, anytime, for anyone who would listen. Their free shows at Central City Park in Macon and Atlanta's Piedmont Park soon became legendary for the sheer intensity of the music. When playing live, it was clear that the sum was even greater than the formidable parts of the Allman Brothers. They were a band—a band that created dynamic, visceral music that no group had played before."

Whether in Macon, Atlanta, or at other stops on tours, people who came to see them perform were blown away. These were the days before CDs, MP3 players, and iPods. Though the quality of sound recordings had come a long way by the early 1970s, many **nuances** were available only when listening to a group in person. That was true of the Allman Brothers Band. Concertgoers were entranced by the dual guitar work of Duane and Dickey, complemented by Berry's bass line and Jaimoe and Butch on drums. Then there was Gregg. In person, his vocals and organ work were even more evident. Slide guitar was something alien to many rock fans, but with Duane's skillful playing, they could appreciate the role it played in the group's music.

But it wasn't just those things that made an Allman Brothers Band concert something better than what could be achieved in a recording studio, no matter how technologically advanced the recording equipment was. Band members fed off the enthusiasm of the crowd. The crowd got enthusiastic, and the band's energy level increased. Fans yelled their approval of a guitar "duel," and Duane and Dickey were more than happy to keep it going. Allman Brothers Band concerts were mutually beneficial: the musicians enjoyed them as much as the fans did.

Back to the Studio

In 1970, the Allman Brothers Band returned to the Capricorn studios in Macon to cut another album. This time, the group found the right combination, and *Idlewild South* was a big hit with the group's fans. Critics again sang the praises of the band.

Idlewild South was named after a ranch near Macon. Thom "Ace" Doucette was a guest artist on the album, playing the harmonica and

Whether singing while playing the guitar or performing on the keyboards, Gregg captivated the audience. The audience was able to hear sounds that those whose only exposure to the band was from records could not. No matter how good the album was, to truly experience the Allman Brothers Band required that one see them in concert.

tambourine. With this album, Dickey and Gregg showed another talent they both possessed—as songwriters; between them, they wrote all but one of the album's tracks. Dickey wrote "Revival," one of the album's most popular songs. Gregg created "Midnight Rider," another popular song from the album.

Dickey is also responsible for writing the group's first instrumental song, "In Memory of Elizabeth Reed." The jazz- and Latin-influenced song became a staple at Allman Brothers Band concerts, and it also became the subject of one of the great mysteries of the group. The title of the song comes from a tombstone at Rose Hill Cemetery, where Dickey sometimes went to write. According to legends that surround the group, that wasn't the only thing Dickey did there. He will admit that the title came from the tombstone of Elizabeth Reed Napier, but he's cagey about the rest. According to most, the song was inspired by a relationship Dickey had with a woman whose name he couldn't reveal. There are some, however, who claim that he wrote the song after he took a girl to the cemetery and "got romantic" near the tombstone. He strongly denies that version of the tale.

Whatever the inspiration for the album and its songs, it was a critical and commercial success. Important to album sales was the radio airplay its songs received. According to *Rolling Stone*, that was a significant factor in the album's success. *Idlewild South* contained songs more likely to be played on radio. Songs like "Midnight Rider" were short enough to receive radio play. Often, songs by the Allman Brothers Band would go on . . . and on . . . and on. Radio stations across the country didn't want lengthy songs, no matter how good they were. The songs that received the most airplay were generally two or three minutes in length. The Allman Brothers Band tended to like longer songs; it gave the guys time to showcase their talents. But, with *Idlewild South*, the group's songs appeared more frequently on radio playlists, gaining fans throughout the country—and, giving birth to a new music **genre**.

The Birth of Southern Rock

> **Home Grown**
> **Deep Fried and Sanctified**
> **A Little Bluesy, a Little Bit of Soul**
> **and a Whole Lot of Country Attitude.**

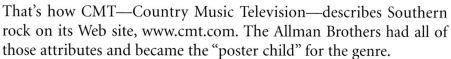

That's how CMT—Country Music Television—describes Southern rock on its Web site, www.cmt.com. The Allman Brothers had all of those attributes and became the "poster child" for the genre.

Little Richard, Bo Diddley, Jerry Lee Lewis, and Elvis Presley were some of the biggest pioneers in rock music in the 1950s and 1960s. Besides their talent, they and many of the other early rock musicians shared something else: they came from the South. Then came the Beatles, the Rolling Stones, the Yardbirds, and the other

Not only was news of the Allman Brothers Band's talent spreading, but the band also brought a new genre to the fans—Southern rock. Before long, listeners everywhere would associate the band with this new style of music. In this photo, Gregg and Duane are shown in a performance of what some in the music industry called "deep fried and sanctified."

groups associated with the British Invasion, and the sounds that had come from the South were put aside in favor of the new kids in town. But by the late 1960s and the early 1970s, music coming from the South again captured the interest of the listening public. Ironically, Creedence Clearwater Revival, a band from northern California, and The Band, from Canada, were instrumental in the resurgence of interest in the original form of rock—and it wasn't what was coming from Britain. The roots of rock were in the blues and soul of the South, in places like Muscle Shoals, Alabama, and Macon, Georgia, and the Allman Brothers Band was one of the first to embrace its Southern roots, incorporate them into its sound, and be successful doing so.

The Allman Brothers Band and Southern Rock

Early Southern rock took elements of rock, soul, country, and blues to create its recognizable sound. The rock that came out of places like Muscle Shoals, Alabama, and Macon, Georgia, during the 1970s, however, wasn't the same as that performed during its early days a decade or two before. The new Southern rock, performed by groups such as the Marshall Tucker Band, the Elvin Bishop Band, as well as the Allman Brothers Band, added influences of country and folk music to the blues, rock, and soul. Strong instrumental performances, especially on the guitar, were important. For the Allman Brothers Band, Duane on the slide guitar, an instrument closely associated with country music, became a large part of the group's signature sound.

The vocalist was extremely important to early Southern rock, and vocals remained important in its reemergence. In fact, the vocalist sometimes "made" the song. Gregg's raspy, sometimes gruff vocal styling and Charlie Daniel's monotones might not have worked for popular rock songs, but for Southern rock, they were perfect and quickly became identifiable with that genre.

Another characteristic of Southern rock was extended playing times, especially during live performances. In other words, Southern rock bands, like the Allman Brothers Band, could take a single song and turn it into a forty-minute performance. It seemed as though once Dicky, Berry, and Duane, or Jaimoe and Butch got started, there was no stopping them. Concert performances turned into what felt

The Allman Brothers Band had a unique sound, and much of the credit for that goes to Duane's skill on the slide guitar. The slide guitar was relatively new to rock music, and no rocker had used it as extensively as Duane and the Allman Brothers Band. The guitar could be played either when held traditionally or when held horizontally.

like intimate jam sessions—in front of thousands of their closest and admiring friends!

It Wasn't All Southern Glory

The problem with labels is that they lump people—and rock groups—together based on just a few characteristics. Some groups called Southern rock didn't like being labeled. Gregg even said,

Rock . . . Southern rock . . . the members of the Allman Brothers Band really didn't care what their music was called. They just wanted to play their music. So they did. The Allman Brothers Band traveled, recorded, and put its music out there for people to hear. And the people loved it—no matter what it was called.

"Southern rock is a bit redundant; it's like saying rock rock." To him, the Allman Brothers Band was a rock band, and that was fine.

Some labels deal with much more serious issues. One such label was "racist"; some people perceived Southern rock bands as being prejudiced against black Americans. Battles fought on behalf of the civil rights movement were fresh in the minds of many. Media coverage of people, even children, being attacked by police dogs and sprayed with fire hoses spread across the country. The violent deaths of the Reverend Dr. Martin Luther King Jr. in Tennessee, civil rights workers James Chaney, Andrew Goodman, and Michael Schwerner in Mississippi, and the bombing deaths of four young girls—Carole Denise McNair, Addie Mae Collins, Cynthia Welsey, and Carol Robertson—in an Alabama church sickened many all over the country. And into this **volatile** time came a music style that seemed to celebrate the racist history that was a part of the South for so many years. Some of the groups proudly displayed what many consider to be one of the oldest symbols of racism in the country—the Confederate flag.

Sometimes the perceptions came as a result of something bands and their members could not control. For some Southern rock bands, the Confederate flag became part of their image, whether or not they liked it. Often, as in the case of Lynyrd Skynyrd and the Allman Brothers Band, the decision to make that association came from their record labels. In a 1995 interview in *Knight Ridder Tribune*, Dickey talked about the group and the flag:

> **"Our record company started putting these flags on our posters back in the '70s, and we had to tell them 'We're not Rebels. We're not bigots.' We're not rednecks, for God's sake. It's like they were aligning us with the . . . Civil War."**

Allen Woody, who joined the band in 1989, said in the same interview:

> **"The thing that hangs over us that's irritating is the whole Rebel flag thing. I'm proud to be from the South, and I'm proud our band is from the South. But there are certain elements of Southern history that**

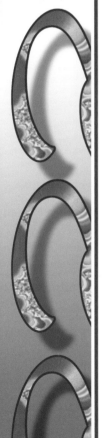

I don't want to be associated with, if you know what I mean.**"**

Though some groups, like Lynyrd Skynyrd and Black Oak Arkansas, seemed to play up the idea that their members were racists and rednecks, that wasn't the Allman Brothers Band's style. Yes, the Confederate flag was displayed on album covers, but that had been Capricorn's decision, not the band's. More important, the

Not all symbols of the South were associated with good things. One such symbol was the Confederate flag. The record companies for whom the Allman Brothers Band and Lynyrd Skynyrd (shown in this photo) cut their tracks began using the flag on the groups' albums and as backdrops. Many Americans then associated the flag's negative connotations with the groups.

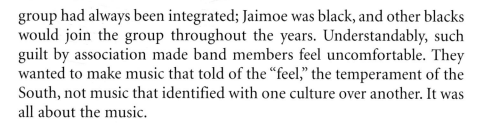

group had always been integrated; Jaimoe was black, and other blacks would join the group throughout the years. Understandably, such guilt by association made band members feel uncomfortable. They wanted to make music that told of the "feel," the temperament of the South, not music that identified with one culture over another. It was all about the music.

Success

The year 1970 had been a good one for the Allman Brothers Band. Critics loved the group, and more and more people were quickly becoming fans. The guys had found the key to getting radio airplay, and their songs were now heard all over the country. They had found success, and they were loving every minute of it, even though Duane pushed them all hard so they could do their best.

Individual success was also in the cards for Duane during 1970. He hooked up with Eric Clapton and Derek and the Dominoes. When their album *Layla and Other Assorted Love Songs* was released in 1970, Duane's reputation as a guitar genius was assured. Eric Clapton's reputation as a guitarist is stellar as well, and when the two got together on the album, it was magic. According to some critics, that album is the best guitar album ever released. And as Duane's reputation as a guitarist grew, interest in the Allman Brothers Band increased. Music lovers, especially those who loved guitar, wanted to hear everything Duane did. It was a win-win situation.

With the successful year of 1970 behind them, the Allman Brothers Band looked forward to an even better 1971. Little did anyone know that their entire world—personal and professional—would be rocked to its very foundation.

The Allman Brothers Band was hot, and they needed to record a live album. *At the Fillmore East* was a huge hit and became the group's first gold record. Some historians claim there is a direct relationship between its success and the ability of other Southern rock bands to make it big.

4

Ups and Downs

One of the most important names during the early days of rock was not a singer or musician. It was Bill Graham, a record promoter. Artists wanting to make it in the rock world dreamed of being noticed by Bill and having the opportunity to perform at his Fillmore East in New York City, or at San Francisco's Fillmore West.

Big names played at both Fillmores. The Doors and the Grateful Dead were regulars at Fillmore West. The Grateful Dead also played at Fillmore East. Others who found their way to the East Village club included The Who, Jimi Hendrix, Led Zeppelin, Neil Young and Crazy Horse, and Pink Floyd. The Allman Brothers Band were sometimes referred to as "Bill Graham's House Band" because they played at the Fillmore East so many times.

The Allman Brothers Band and the Fillmore East

The group knew it had to take advantage of the success it had achieved with *Idlewild South* and record another album. They wanted this album to be special, so they decided to record a live album. Fillmore East had been the site of live recordings by several other groups, and

Being a big rock star in the 1960s and 1970s usually meant playing at the Fillmore East (shown in this photo) or the Fillmore West. The Allman Brothers Band was a regular at the Fillmore East. When the club closed in 1971, the Allman Brothers Band was the last band to perform.

for the Allman Brothers Band, it must have felt almost as comfortable performing there as it did recording at Capricorn in Macon.

They decided their first live album would be recorded during two March 1971 performances at Fillmore East. Many music critics have called what came out of those sessions, *At Fillmore East*, one of the best live albums of all time. The album prompted *Rolling Stone* to call the Allman Brothers "the best . . . band in the country."

Apparently fans agreed and bought the album in droves. *At the Fillmore East* became the group's first gold album. Fans loved the guitar interplay between Duane and Dickey. Berry's bass and Gregg's vocals, which reminded some of Ray Charles, and expertise on the organ added to the band's rich sounds. Songs included a **cover** of "Statesboro Blues" (originally done by Blind Willie McTell), "Whipping Post," and a new, haunting version of "In Memory of Elizabeth Reed" (and Dickey still wasn't coming clean on who the song was *really* about). The album shot up the charts, and its success caused interest in Southern rock to increase as well. According to some music historians, the success of *At the Fillmore East* was what led bands such as the Marshall Tucker Band and Lynyrd Skynyrd to break out and become successful.

In June 1971, Bill Graham closed the Fillmore East. Clubs such as the Fillmore East and Fillmore West had been important during rock's early days. But times had changed, and concerts had become the way most people saw their favorite groups. It was time to say good-bye to Fillmore East. Among those invited to play one final time at the club were Frank Zappa and the Mothers of Invention and the Beach Boys. Befitting their status as frequent performers, the Allman Brothers Band was invited to be the last group to perform. And they didn't disappoint, playing all night. In a 2005 interview, Gregg said the reason they did so was simple: they were having so much fun jamming, they lost track of time. When someone opened the side door of the club and they could see the sun was up, they realized they had played straight through until morning.

"The Sky Is Crying"

Building on the success of *At the Fillmore East*, the Allman Brothers Band spent much of 1971 touring. With each performance, crowds were bigger and more enthusiastic. Drinking in that enthusiasm, the guys poured their hearts and souls into each performance. Soon, though, the band started working on their third album, hoping to surpass the success of *At the Fillmore.*

The future looked bright for the Allman Brothers Band—but that changed quickly for the band on October 29, 1971. On his way home from a birthday party for Berry's wife, Duane's motorcycle swerved to miss a truck that had pulled out in front of him. He was thrown from the bike and died a few hours later from massive internal injuries. Duane was twenty-four years old.

Family, his fellow band members, friends, and fans were in a state of shock. It didn't seem fair; he was young, talented, and just beginning to taste success. Phil Walden, the group's manager, described the loss of Duane Allman, musician and friend:

> **"Duane Allman's death is a very personal loss, not only for the no-nonsense, straight-ahead music he created, but for the warm and sincere friendship we shared. To remember Duane is to recall his music, and that exactly is what the man was all about."**

Johnny Sandlin of Capricorn Records, and a former member of Hour Glass, said,

> **"More than anyone else, Duane Allman was responsible for the musical revolution in the South."**

More than three hundred attended Duane's funeral. As the surviving band members and Thom "Ace" Doucette began to play in his honor, Gregg sang in his soulful, emotion-filled voice, "The sky is crying, look at the tears roll down my cheeks."

Duane was buried in Macon's Rose Hill Cemetery.

Moving On

As hard as it was for the band to move on, the members knew that's what they had to do. It's what Duane would have wanted the band to do; it had always been about the music. At the time of Duane's death, the band had been working on its next album. Now the band set out to finish the project, with Dickey picking up where Duane left off.

In 1971, amid the highs that come with success, tragedy struck the Allman Brothers Band and the music world. At the age of twenty-four, Duane Allman was killed in a motorcycle accident. More than three hundred people who knew and loved him attended his funeral to celebrate his life and to say good-bye.

The result, the double album *Eat a Peach*, is considered an Allman Brothers Band classic. Some critics have hailed the album as showing the group at the height of its musical brilliance. Music writer Greil Marcus described the album as being an

"after-the-rain celebration . . . ageless, seamless . . . front porch music stolen from the utopia of shared southern memory."

The album title comes from a radio interview Duane once gave. When the interviewer asked him what he was doing in terms of protest, Duane responded: "There ain't no revolution, it's evolution, but every time I'm in Georgia I eat a peach for peace."

Eat a Peach, released in 1972, is a combination of tracks the band laid down in sessions just before Duane's death and songs recorded during the group's live sessions for *At the Fillmore*. Included on the album are songs that have become Allman Brothers Band fan favorites—"Melissa," "Ain't Wastin' Time No More," "Blue Sky," and the almost-thirty-four minute "Mountain Jam." "Little Martha," an acoustic guitar piece, is named after a gravesite at Rose Hill Ceremony; atop the grave is a statue of a little girl, Little Martha.

New Members—and Lightning Strikes

For a while, the band toured with just five members. Eventually, the group decided to add another keyboardist, and Chuck Leavell joined the group. With a new lineup, the band was eager to perform and anxious to record.

But fate interrupted.

On November 11, 1972, just three blocks from where Duane had been killed the year before, Berry had a motorcycle accident. He told emergency personnel he felt fine, and he went home rather than to the hospital. A few hours later, Berry died, the result of a skull fracture. He was buried in Rose Hill Cemetery, next to Duane.

The group had not replaced Duane, but it had to replace Berry. It couldn't go on and play the type of music it wanted to without a bass player. In December 1972, Lamar Williams, a long-time friend of Jaimoe's, joined the group to play bass, and the group continued work on its next album.

They were professionals, so the members of the Allman Brothers Band set aside their pain and continued making music. Instead of finding someone to assume Duane's role with the group, the band decided to make a go of it with just five members. In this photo, the guys make a rest stop during a bus tour.

The Top

As tragic and unforgettable as 1971 and 1972 had been, 1973 began with promise. The Allman Brothers Band continued to tour, and by 1973, it had become one of the highest-grossing concert groups in the United States. In July, the band joined the Grateful Dead and The Band to perform at Summer Jam, a concert held at Watkins Glen raceway, outside the town of Watkins Glen, New York. An estimated crowd of 600,000 people flocked to the racetrack for the festival.

The following month, *Brothers and Sisters* came out. It shot straight to the #1 spot on the album charts. The album stayed on the charts for more than a year. The album had a more country sound than previous recordings, something most music writers claim shows Dickey's growing leadership. Included on the album were "Jessica," an instrumental song, and "Ramblin' Man," written by Dickey, which reached #2 on the charts. Despite the tragedy of the preceding two years, the band had regrouped and come out stronger than ever. To

By 1973, few groups could touch the Allman Brothers Band as a touring group. Its concerts brought in more money than most other groups' appearances. In July of that year, the Allman Brothers Band, the Grateful Dead, and the Band played before 600,000 fans at Summer Jam, near Watkins Glen, New York.

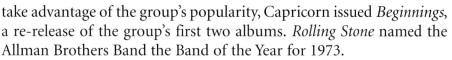

take advantage of the group's popularity, Capricorn issued *Beginnings,* a re-release of the group's first two albums. *Rolling Stone* named the Allman Brothers Band the Band of the Year for 1973.

December 31, 1973, was also a milestone for the band. Long-time friend, promoter Bill Graham arranged for a nationwide broadcast of the concert the group was giving in San Francisco. Jerry Garcia and Bill Kreutzmann of the Grateful Dead and Boz Skaggs, a friend from Muscle Shoals days, sat in with the group.

Nowhere to Go

People closest to the band claim that Berry was the person who had held the guys together, keeping them focused on the same goal after Duane died. With Berry gone, the band lost its anchor.

As if that wasn't enough, the downside of fame and the money that comes with it began to affect the guys. When Duane and Berry were there, providing direction, everyone seemed to have the same goal—making good music. Now, without them, other interests were beginning to consume the surviving members of the Allman Brothers Band. Gregg and Dickey did some solo work. Gregg's first solo release, a soul- and gospel-influenced album *Laid Back,* was a critical success. He followed the album's release with a successful tour and a live solo album. Some people suspected that Gregg's success as a solo artist threatened some of the other band members.

And then there was Cher.

Sonny and Cher were pop music legends. Everyone—not just music fans—knew the couple. But in 1975, their marriage ended. Just a few days after Cher's divorce from her long-time husband Sonny Bono became final, she and Gregg were married. Ten days after the wedding, Cher filed for divorce. Then the couple reconciled. Then they separated. And reconciled. Had a baby, Elijah Blue. Separated. Though the marriage officially lasted from 1975 until 1979, they spent very little time together.

Gregg's on-again-off-again marriage strained his relationship with the other band members. They still toured and made music, and sometimes it was good. But other times, the tensions among band members compromised the quality of the music. Chuck and Dickey had different ideas about the direction the group's music should go. The focus became increasingly lost, and the group's next album, *Win,*

FEAR GRIPS HOLLYWOOD!
MANSON GANG STILL ON THE LOOSE!

EXCLUSIVE INTERVIEW
WITH TONY ORLANDO!

CC 02414

JANUARY 60¢

Screen Stars

They're At A Madman's Mercy...
CHER & CHASTITY TERRORIZED!
GREGG ALMOST KILLED!
Police Have No Clues!

In one of the most unusual marriages in rock history, Gregg and Cher got married. But it wasn't a happy relationship. Though their marriage would legally last until 1979, they spent little time together. The marriage produced two things: a son, Elijah Blue, and conflict within the Allman Brothers Band.

Lose or Draw, released in 1975, was a disappointment. Critics point out some highlights on the album, including "High Falls," but overall they consider the album "uninspired." The band members who used to spend countless hours together began to spend less and less time together until they were basically together only during shows. Perhaps as a sign of wishful thinking, Capricorn released a compilation album, *The Road Goes on Forever*, in 1975. But the road was about to come to an end for the Allman Brothers Band.

The Bottom

Not too many people were surprised when Gregg was arrested on federal drug charges in 1976. There had long been stories about Gregg's drug use, especially his addiction to heroin. After his arrest, Gregg made a deal with authorities in which he'd testify against his road manager, Scooter Herring. Scooter was convicted for narcotics trafficking and sentenced to seventy-five years in prison.

For the others in the group, that was the end of their involvement with the surviving Allman brother. By testifying against a band family member, Gregg had broken the loyalty that had held the group together. Dickey went off to work on his solo career, and Jaimoe, Chuck, and Lamar formed Sea Level. The four swore they would never work with Gregg again.

After the release of another album, which sold poorly, the guys decided to make their split official. The reign of the Allman Brothers Band was over.

The relationship between members of the Allman Brothers Band was a lot like Gregg's marriage to Cher—together, apart, and together, apart, together. A drug bust had contributed to the breakup of the band, but it seemed as though the guys (at least some of them) were meant to be together.

5

Reformed and Re-Formed

T he guys had trouble staying completely away from each other. Maybe they had been together too long to stay apart. Perhaps Dickey was right: "We're like a big dysfunctional family, but we get along all right." After a few years, the brotherhood Duane and Berry had nurtured proved too strong for bad feelings to keep most of the guys apart.

On Their Own

During their break, the guys were free to pursue their personal interests. Gregg had his solo work (including an almost universally panned album with Cher), and his continuing battle with drugs and alcohol. He released *Playing Up a Storm*. The album was his biggest on his own.

Besides Gregg, the only other member of the Allman Brothers Band who tasted success during the group's separation was Dickey, who formed a group called Great Southern. The group used the Allman Brothers

Band's recipe for success: two guitars, two drums, keyboards, bass, and vocals. Despite following the lead of a proven winner, Great Southern had only marginal success.

Together Again

In 1978, Gregg, Butch, Dickey, and Jaimoe began talking about reviving the Allman Brothers Band. None had reached the same solo success that had seemed at times almost effortless with the Allman Brothers Band. Because Chuck and Lamar wanted to stay with Sea Level, Great Southern members Dan Toler was chosen to play guitar and David "Rook" Goldflies to play bass.

In 1979, the re-formed band released *Enlightened Rogue.* "Crazy Love" was a hit single, but overall, the album was only a moderate success. During the group's "intermission," it had lost much of its fan base.

On top of a lack of popularity, the band also had problems with their record company. The Allman Brothers Band had been part of the Capricorn family from the beginning. But with the decrease in the band's popularity came financial problems for the label and for the band. In 1979, Capricorn failed, and PolyGram bought the label's catalogue. For the first time in its existence, the Allman Brothers Band found itself recording for another label—Arista. The group responded to the label change with two albums that were slammed by the critics. More important, the albums weren't purchased by music lovers either. Jaimoe was fired and Dan's brother David hired to play drums. Mike Lawler was brought on board to play keyboards. But the situation didn't improve. By early 1982, this edition of the Allman Brothers Band was history.

Apart Again

It didn't take long for Gregg and Dickey to pick up on their other recording careers. Gregg formed the Gregg Allman Band with the Tolers and made the rounds of small venues. Dickey eventually formed the Dickey Betts Band.

In 1986, the Allman Brothers Band reunited for two benefit concerts. Though the performance was painless, there was no talk of reunion among the members. In 1987, the Gregg Allman Band and the Dickey Betts Band played a club tour. Each band played its own set, and at the end, the bands came together to sing a set consisting of Allman Brothers Band hits. Over the next few years, the Gregg Allman

During one of the "apart times," Gregg formed the Gregg Allman Band. Though it didn't have the success of the Allman Brothers Band, the band wasn't a failure. When the Gregg Allman Band played some sets with the Dickey Betts Band, rumors flew that the Allman Brothers Band would reunite.

Band and the Dickey Bets Band worked together on projects more and more frequently. In 1989, the inevitable happened—the Allman Brothers Band reunited . . . again.

Not Just Dreams

By 1989, radio had changed, or rather, what was being played on radio stations across the country changed. Station programmers looked to established band for their playlists. Bands like the Rolling Stones, Jefferson Airplane, The Who, and the Allman Brothers Band all saw resurgences in their popularity. In 1989, PolyGram released a compilation box set *Dreams*, which received critical raves and was financially successful.

When the Allman Brothers Band reunited in 1989, there was an audience eager for their music. Members of the band were now Johnny Neel on keyboards and harmonica, Allen Woody on bass, Gregg, Dickey, Jaimoe, and Butch. Leavell decided to stick with session work and touring with the Rolling Stones.

One of the new members was Warren Haynes on guitar. Dickey had selected Warren for his band during one of the Allman Brothers Band's breaks. According to Dickey, Warren was the first slide-guitarist he felt comfortable playing with since Duane. Dickey spoke of Warren's talents in a 1995 interview:

> **"What I like about Warren, is that he can stand there night after night and be hit in the head with that sound of mine and not start sounding like me. He's got his own style. It's unique. . . . he's good."**

The band returned to what it knew very well—touring. The Allman Brothers Band became regulars on summer outdoor tours. Their concerts were well-received, and as had happened in the group's early days, the members found themselves playing before larger and larger crowds. They might not have been as big as they had in the early days, but for this edition of the Allman Brothers Band, the crowds were big enough to keep them excited and enthusiastic about their music.

The Nineties and Memories Rekindled

The 1990s began with a new record label for the band—Epic—and this time the releases were successful. Of course things couldn't go completely without bumps in the road, and the decade brought the departure of Warren, Woody, and Johnny. Marc Quinones joined the band, as did Oteil Brubridge and Derek Trucks, Butch's nephew.

Of course one of the biggest highlights of the decade for the band was its induction into the Rock and Roll Hall of Fame. Unlike some groups for whom it takes five, six, even eight nominations before they are voted in (if at all), the Allman Brothers Band made it in its first year of eligibility.

In 1996, the band won its first and only Grammy Award when "Jessica" won the Best Rock Instrumental Performance. Dickey wrote the song for his daughter Jessica.

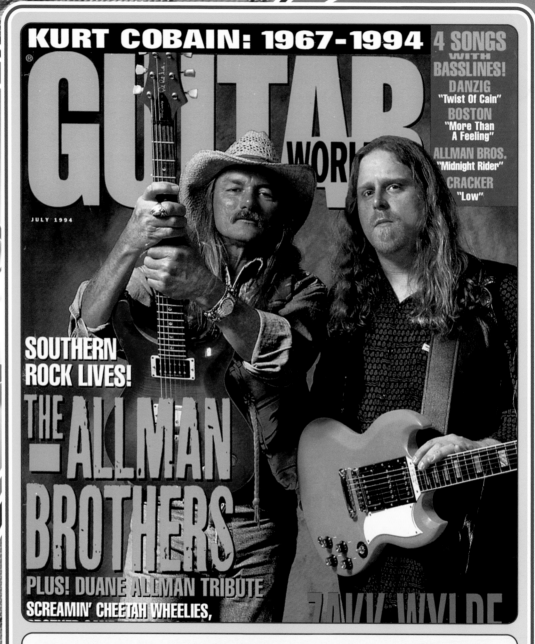

KURT COBAIN: 1967-1994

GUITAR WORLD

JULY 1994

4 SONGS WITH BASSLINES!
DANZIG "Twist Of Cain"
BOSTON "More Than A Feeling"
ALLMAN BROS. "Midnight Rider"
CRACKER "Low"

SOUTHERN ROCK LIVES!
THE ALLMAN BROTHERS
PLUS! DUANE ALLMAN TRIBUTE
SCREAMIN' CHEETAH WHEELIES,
ZAKK WYLDE

When the Allman Brothers Band reconciled in 1989, a new guy was on guitar—Warren Haynes. Warren had played in one of Dickey's groups, and Dickey wanted him in the newest version of the Allman Brothers Band. Dickey (left) and Warren (right) talked about the group in the July 1994 issue of *Guitar World*.

Individually, Gregg spread his wings into another venture—acting—in 1991. He appeared in the hit film *Rush*. He also "appeared" in the animated television show *The Family Guy*. More important than that or the success of the band, Gregg got sober, quitting heroin and alcohol cold turkey and developing a new spirituality.

As successful and promising as the 1990s were, the decade also brought back memories of some of the band's darkest days. In 1998, the Georgia state legislature voted to designate the part of State Highway 19 that goes through the city of Macon as Duane Allman Boulevard. That year the legislature also passed a resolution renaming a bridge on that highway as the Raymond Berry Oakley III Bridge.

Members have come and gone and two of its best has died. Still, the Allman Brothers Band has continued to exist and perform. It tours regularly and even inspired a hit movie. Eager fans attend its concerts and buy its CDs. The Allman Brothers Band's fans might be multigenerational, but they have the love of the group in common.

A New Millennium

The new millennium brought new music, new tours, and new problems. Before undertaking its summer 2000 tour, the band "asked" Dickey to sit that one out. Personal problems were affecting his professional life, and the other band members felt Dickey needed to concentrate on solving them; then he could come back to the band. But that wasn't to happen. Dickey filed a lawsuit against the surviving members of the original Allman Brothers Band. Dickey's departure from the group was permanent. Although Dickey left the band, Warren Haynes began playing with the guys again in 2000.

In 2000, the group released a live CD called *Peakin' at the Beacon.* New York's Beacon Theater has been the site of more than 200 concerts by the Allman Brothers. Fans still flock to the theater each March to hear the group.

Awards and Accolades

In 2003, awards and honors were bestowed on the group as a whole and to its members, past and present. "Instrumental Illness" brought the group Grammy nominations in 2003 and 2004. Also in 2003, *Rolling Stone* named Duane the #2 greatest guitarist of all time; Jimi Hendrix claimed the top spot. Other members of the Allman Brothers Band with spots on the list were Warren Haynes (#23), Dickey Betts (#58), and Derek Trucks (#81). In 2004, *Rolling Stone* named the group #52 on its list of the of the 100 Greatest Artists of All Time.

In 2006, the television network CMT compiled its list of the twenty greatest Southern rock songs. At #2, behind Lynyrd Skynyrd's Southern rock anthem "Sweet Home Alabama," was the Allman Brothers Band's "Ramblin' Man." "Midnight Rider" came in at #6. Gregg's solo "I'm No Angel" rounded out the top twenty.

Gregg also received a personal honor in 2006 when he was named to the Georgia Hall of Fame.

Despite a sometimes-rocky path, the band continues to play together and separately. Every year, for example, the guys make an appearance at the Wanee Music Festival in Florida. Gregg Allman and Friends performed in Hawaii in early 2007. They've had numerous ups and downs—but their continuing popularity makes them true rock legends.

1961   Gregg and Duane Allman begin their musical careers playing in garage bands around Jacksonville and Daytona Beach.

1969   **March 25**   The Allman Brothers Band is officially formed.

The group's debut album, *The Allman Brothers Band*, is released to critical praise.

1970   The Allman Brothers Band plays more than 300 shows.

The group's second album, *Idlewild South*, is released and becomes its first major hit with fans.

Duane Allman records with Eric Clapton, solidifying his reputation as a guitar genius.

1971   **March**   The group records performances at Fillmore East that will become its first live album.

June   The group becomes the last one to play at Fillmore East.

October 29   Duane Allman is killed in a motorcycle accident.

1972   *Eat a Peach* is released, a combination of Duane's last tracks and songs from the Fillmore show.

November 11   Berry Oakley dies from injuries received in a motorcycle accident.

1973   **July**   The group joins the Grateful Dead and The Band to perform at Summer Jam outside Watkins Glen, New York.

September   *Brothers and Sisters* is released and shoots to #1. It will stay on the charts for a year.

December 31   Friend and rock promoter Bill Graham arranges for a nationwide broadcast of the concert the group gives in San Francisco.

The Allman Brothers Band becomes one of he highest-grossing concert groups in the United States.

Rolling Stone names the Allman Brothers Band the Band of the Year for 1973.

1975   Gregg marries Cher of the famous Sonny and Cher rock duo.

Win, Lose or Draw is released and considered a weak effort.

1976   Gregg is arrested on federal drug charges.

The Allman Brothers Band breaks up.

1978 Talks begin among Gregg, Butch, Dickey, and Jaimoe to re-form the group.

1979 Gregg and Cher are officially divorced.

The re-formed Allman Brothers Band releases *Enlightened Rogue*.

1982 The Allman Brothers Band dissolves.

1986 The band regroups for two benefit concerts.

1987 The Gregg Allman Band and the Dickey Betts Band play a club tour.

1989 The Allman Brothers Band reunites and begins its series of performances at the Beacon.

1991 Gregg begins acting, appearing in *Rush* and other projects.

1995 **January 13** The Allman Brothers Band is inducted into the Rock and Roll Hall of Fame.

September The Allman Brothers Band plays at the grand opening of the Rock and Roll Hall of Fame in Cleveland, Ohio.

1996 The band wins its first and only Grammy Award.

1998 The Georgia state legislature designates the part of State Highway 19 that goes through the city of Macon as Duane Allman Boulevard. A bridge on that highway is named the Raymond Berry Oakley III Bridge.

2000 The band "asks" Dickey to skip the summer tour.

2003 "Instrumental Illness" brings the group a Grammy nomination.

Rolling Stone names Duane Allman, Warren Haynes, Dickey Betts, and Derek Trucks to its "Greatest Guitarist" list.

2004 "Instrumental Illness" bring the group another Grammy nomination.

Rolling Stone names the Allman Brothers Band #52 on its list of the 100 Greatest Artists of All Time.

2006 CMT names "Ramblin' Man" and "Midnight Rider" to its Top-20 Southern Rock Songs. Gregg's solo "I'm No Angel" rounds out the top twenty.

Gregg is inducted into the Georgia Hall of Fame.

Albums

1969   *The Allman Brothers Band*

1970   *Idlewild South*

1971   *At Fillmore East*

1972   *Eat a Peach*

1973   *Brothers and Sisters*
       Beginnings

1975   *Win, Lose or Draw*
       The Road Goes on Forever

1976   *Wipe the Windows, Check the Oil, Dollar Gas*

1978   *Statesboro Blues*

1979   *Enlightened Rogues*

1980   *Reach for the Sky*

1981   *Brothers of the Road*

1989   *Dreams*

1990   *Seven Turns*

1991   *Shades of Two Worlds*
       Live at Ludlow Garage: 1970
       A Decade of Hits 1969–1979

1992   *An Evening with the Allman Brothers Band: First Set*
       Ramblin' Man

1994   *Where It All Began*

1995   *Legendary Hits*
       An Evening with the Allman Brothers Band: Second Set

1996   *Fillmore East, February 1970*

1998   *Mycology: An Anthology*

2000   *Peakin' at the Beacon*
       20th Century Masters—The Millennium Collection:
         The Best of the Allman Brothers Band

2002   *American University 12/13/70*
       Still Rockin'

2003 *Martin Scorsese Presents the Blues: The Allman Brothers*
Hittin' the Note
Live at the Atlanta International Pop Festival: July 3 & 5, 1970
S.U.N.Y. at Stonybrook: Stonybrook, NY 9/19/71

2004 *Stand Back: The Anthology*
The Essential Allman Brothers Band: The Epic Years
One Way Out
Macon City Auditorium: 2/11/72

2005 *Nassau Coliseum, Uniondale, NY: 5/1/73*
Gold

2006 *Essential*

Videos

1982 *Brothers of the Road*

2002 *Best of the Allman Brothers Band*

2003 *Live in Gainesville*
The Allman Brothers Band—Live at the Beacon

Awards and Recognitions

1995 Inducted into the Rock and Roll Hall of Fame.

1996 Grammy Award: Best Rock Instrumental Performance ("Jessica").

1998 Georgia State Legislature: Part of State Highway 19 and a bridge renamed in honor of Duane Allman and Berry Oakley.

2003 Grammy Award: Best Rock Instrumental Performance, nominated ("Instrumental Illness").

Rolling Stone: Duane Allman, Warren Haynes, Dickey Betts, and Derek Trucks named to its "Greatest Guitarists" list.

2004 Grammy Award: Best Rock Instrumental Performance, nominated ("Instrumental Illness").

Rolling Stone: The Allman Brothers Band is ranked #52 on its list of the 100 Greatest Artists of All Time.

2006 CMT: "Ramblin' Man" and "Midnight Rider" are named to its Top-20 Southern Rock Songs.

Gregg Allman is inducted into the Georgia Hall of Fame.

Books

Freeman, Scott, and Mark Chimsky. *Midnight Riders: The Story of the Allman Brothers Band.* New York: Little, Brown, 1996.

Kemp, Mark. *Dixie Lullaby.* Athens: University of Georgia Press, 2006.

McStravick, Summer, and John Roos (eds.). *Blues-Rock Explosion: From the Allman Brothers to the Yardbirds.* Mission Viejo, Calif.: Old Goat Publishing, 2002.

Patterson, R. Gary. *Take a Walk on the Dark Side: Rock and Roll Myths, Legends, and Curses.* New York: Simon and Schuster, 2004.

Perkins, William. *No Saints, No Saviors: My Years with the Allman Brothers Band.* Macon, Ga.: Mercer University Press, 2005.

Poe, Randy. *Skydog: The Duane Allman Story.* San Mateo, Calif.: Music Player Network, 2006.

Rubin, Dave. *Best of Southern Rock.* Milwaukee, Wis.: Hal Leonard, 2002.

Web Sites

www.allmanbrothersband.com
Hittin' the Web with the Allman Brothers Band

www.gabba.org
The Georgia Allman Brothers Band Association

www.greggallman.com
Hittin' the Web with Gregg Allman

www.rockhall.com
Rock and Roll Hall of Fame

www.thebighousemuseum.org
The Big House—The Allman Brothers Band Museum

acoustic—Music or a musical instrument that is not amplified.

blues—A type of music that developed from African American folk songs in the early twentieth century, consisting mainly of slow, sad songs.

bossa-nova—A lively form of music and dance that is similar to the samba.

coiffed—Styled ones hair.

cover—To record a piece of music that someone has already recorded.

criteria—Standards used in making decisions about something.

formidable—Inspiring respect or wonder.

fusion—The merging or blending of two or more things.

genre—The category of an artistic.

improvisation—Creating and performing spontaneously, without preparation.

inducted—Installed into a new position.

nuances—Very slight differences.

scrutiny—Close, careful examination.

soul—A style of African American music with a strong emotional quality, and is related to gospel music and rhythm and blues.

vengeance—Punishment inflicted in return for a wrong.

virtuosity—Great skill or technique.

visceral—Proceeding from instinct rather than for reason.

volatile—Prone to a sudden change.

Peter Gregory is a freelance writer and music lover living in New York.

Picture Credits